Y0-CAS-867

produced 3¼ inches in depth — enough for the present. We were
suffering considerably with drouth. See the 25th inst.

A Swede family, the man a shoe maker, arrived here, & was located at the West Lot.

July, 1863

M. Burnett returned from Indiana. See the 21th ult.
Last night about 100 Federal cavalry encamped in the Office
stable Lot, & we fed them this morning, when they past on to
Hickman Bridge.

A company of rebels entered Harrodsburg last night, and
the neighbors were skedaddling with their horses in every direction
this morning. We hastened beyond the river with ours, where the
Federals have the sway. About noon word came, that the Rebels
had absconded, & quiet was restored.

A little after midnight this morning, a squad of union soldiers
from Danville entered this village, & placed it under guard, ap-
pre'ending that some of the Rebels had taken shelter here, in which
they were quite mistaken. We fed them in the yard, where also they slept.
About 3 o'clock A. M. another squad entered from the north, &
all encamped in the street within the lines, from the cross street to
the forks of the Turnpike Road, the men sleeping in the yards and
lots near the fence by their horses. The first company left in about an
hour; and we furnished breakfast for the balance about 5. A. M.,
when they also left; all went towards Harrodsburg, about 70 or
80 in all.

Amy Runyon deceased of a lingering weakness of many years standing, at the Earl House in her 52th year since the 25th of last August.
She was raised in the Church from infancy, & was an ornament to Society to the day of her death; & will doubtless continue to be so in the
realms of bliss.

J. R. Bryant went to Cincinnati. B. B. Dunlavy & Polly M. Rupe

Pleasant Hill

in the

Civil War

by
THOMAS D. CLARK

Pleasant Hill Press
1972

Printed in the United States of America
by Keystone Printery of Lexington, Kentucky

Contents

Addendum
A Brief Summary of the Shakers at Pleasant Hill
from 1805 to the dissolution of the Society in 1910.

Illustrations

FOREWORD

BY DR. HOLMAN HAMILTON
President
Kentucky Civil War Round Table
(Lexington, Kentucky—450 Members)

Interest in the American Civil War has never flagged. Enthusiasm concerning Civil War incidents, spectacular battles, and prominent leaders is as keen and pervasive in the 1970's as during the Civil War Centennial of 1961-65. Not only academicians but thousands of "amateurs" (many of them actually far from amateurish) write and speak and exchange opinions on developments occurring between the firing on Fort Sumter and the *denouement* at Appomattox. Reliving the conflict on scores of battlefields and visiting other memorable historic sites, associated with wartime leaders, are integral in American tourism. And Civil War Round Tables, in particular, flourish and convincingly symbolize the abiding and widespread interest in "The War."

Equally significant are still other meaningful indices of appreciation of the American heritage. Presidential birthplaces, mansions and cabins and schoolhouses where great and near-great Americans of the past lived and learned and worked, and communities mirroring special features of the American experience are magnets attracting intelligent people. One of the most unusual communities, preserved and restored for grateful members of our own and later generations, is Shakertown at Pleasant Hill, Kentucky, on U. S. 68 between Lexington and Harrodsburg. Here charm and instruction are delightfully combined. And nowhere else is a more serene atmosphere available for those lucky enough to sample and savor it.

This attractive book brings together, in historical retrospect, the Civil War and Pleasant Hill. The author of the contribution, Thomas D. Clark, is both a teacher of note and a skilled writer with a flair for the vivid, dramatic, human, humorous, and homespun. Born in Mississippi in 1903, he received his B.A. degree from the University of Mississippi, the M.A. from the University of Kentucky, and the Ph.D. from Duke University. It is no exaggeration to say that he possesses numerous attributes of cultural statesmanship. The University of Kentucky's Department of History, the University of Kentucky's Margaret I. King Library, the University of Kentucky Press, and later the University Press of Kentucky all were substantially strengthened or indeed envisioned and created by Dr. Clark. Long professor and head of the University of Kentucky's Department of History, he is now distinguished professor of history at Indiana University.

The source material, on which the Clark account is based, consists of the contemporary master journal of events transpiring in the Shaker village of Pleasant Hill between the inception of the Civil War and 1870. Authenticity, therefore, stands out on every page. It is hoped and believed that its reception by the general public will be similar to the pleasure of the Kentucky Civil War Round Table (300 members attended that meeting in Lexington) and subsequently of the Louisville Round Table when those groups heard Clark's oral version.

The text and pictures revive for us the Pleasant Hill of Civil War days. And, as the reader relives the trials and challenges and tribulations of the peace-loving Shaker men and women, he senses something of the poignancy and depth of human problems and achievements in Kentucky long ago.

Acknowledgments

by

JAMES LOWRY COGAR

President, Shakertown at Pleasant Hill, Kentucky, Inc.

Shakertown at Pleasant Hill, Kentucky, Inc., the non-profit educational corporation organized in 1961 to restore the historic Shaker Community at Pleasant Hill, has received many valuable literary contributions but none more important than the original Shaker Civil War Journal presented by Mrs. William Pettit of Lexington, Kentucky.

The Shakers kept meticulous detailed accounts of their daily life and the journal which Mrs. Pettit has given records the days prior to, during, and in the years following the Civil War. This particular journal deals with one of the most tragic periods of this devout sect for the years covered were important ones leading as they did to the final dissolution of the Pleasant Hill experiment in Utopian living.

The journal which covers the years from 1856-1871 was given to Mrs. Pettit by her husband, the late William Pettit, who received it from his kinswomen the noted Kentucky authoress, Nancy Lewis Greene. Miss Greene was the daughter of Dr. Frank M. Greene of Greendale, a prominent Lexington physician. She wrote on many Kentucky subjects and was particularly interested in the Shakers. She spent some of her summers at Pleasant Hill and knew many of the surviving members of the Society. One of her stories is entitled "Ye Olde Shaker Bells" which contains excerpts from the journal. She gives credit to Margaret Buckner Clark for the records she uses, and it is assumed that she received the journal from her.

Out of the exciting material from the Civil War period journal, Dr. Thomas Clark has compiled his interesting account of the Shakers during these trying days.

To Mrs. Pettit we are indebted for her generous gift and to Dr. Clark for writing this narrative of an important and hitherto little known facet of Civil War history.

From a map published in Harper's Weekly in 1862.

Pleasant Hill in the Civil War

by

THOMAS D. CLARK

CHAPTER I

Harvest Years

Kentucky enjoyed its golden decade, 1850-1860. Already long in the past for people were the hardships of pioneering, and that era of beginnings had now become memoirs of old timers, and chapters in Marshall's, Butler's, and Collins' histories of the state. Most of the better lands were now under cultivation, and annually produced abundant crops of all kinds. Hubbard W. Varnon of Bourbon County produced in 1857 more than a hundred bushels of corn per acre on his farm, and the following year the largest business ever was conducted in Louisville in the sale of tobacco. It was a matter of great pride that a Kentucky mule, standing twenty-two and a half hands high, and weighing 2200 pounds, was on public display in Charleston, South Carolina. His record was topped only by *Magnus Appollo,* the Perryville horse, on display in Louisville as the largest horse in the world.

In August, 1853, a sale was held by the Northern Importing Company in which horses, bulls, cows, and blooded sheep were sold at Brutus J. Clay's farm in Bourbon County for staggering prices. This kind of sale was to be repeated several times in the Bluegrass, with farmers stocking their stables and pastures with the best stock available in the British Isles, or from Spain. It was with pride that newspapers reported that in January, 1854, Kentucky exhibitors in the Crystal Palace Exhibition in New York City won the highest awards for native-grown silk, best dressed hank of hemp, for beef, hams, and spiced meats, best manufactured hats and caps, and for Miss Ellen Anderson's patchwork quilt, "Henry Clay."

Evidence of this affluent decade was reflected in the fact that the assessed evaluation of Kentucky property increased $16,000,000 between 1852 and 1853, or reached an all-time high of $33,181,512. This prosperity was to continue down to the outbreak of the Civil War. Immediately following the stifling panic of 1857 Kentucky banks had in circulation $14,345,696 in 1859, and the level was constantly rising.

These were years in which Kentucky's pride was further boosted by success in other areas. The *Belle Key* steamed into Louisville on April 23, 1850, bringing that city within 4 days, 23 hours, and 7 minutes of New Orleans. Three years later the *Eclipse* and the *A. L. Shotwell* bettered the record by 14 hours. While steamboats were reducing the time between the Falls of the Ohio and the greater market city to the south, the race horse *Lexington* defeated the South's wonder horse *LeComte* in an original match, and a second rematch, and then won his owner a heavy purse against his own time record.

In a more than matter-of-fact manner the Ohio River was a busy thoroughfare of commerce. Steamboats crowded in prow-to-prow along the Louisville and Cincinnati water fronts, and ferry boats made hundreds of trips weekly between Covington and Cincinnati. So did those which plied between Louisville and the Indiana towns. In this constant movement went human beings, livestock, and manufactured goods.

It was with marked pride that Kentuckians could look about them in their neighboring states to the west and south and realize that more than 325,000 native sons now lived beyond the Commonwealth's borders. For instance, a majority of Missouri's 100,000 population in 1860 was of Kentucky origin; so were 68,000 Hoosiers, 60,000 Suckers in Illinois, and large numbers of people in Mississippi, Arkansas, and Texas. The stream of population flowed southward from Kentucky with the ever-expanding cotton belt. Both Bluegrass family and place names were strewn across the new frontiers with what appeared abandon. There were Lexingtons, Frankforts, Versailles, Shelbyvilles, and Louisvilles in all the new states.

To boastful sons of this era, Mother Kentucky had become the center of the universe; the keystone of the Republic. Doctrines enunciated by Henry Clay in his "American System" speech were now paying off for his neighbors. Their trade in all directions thrived, and every new year promised to exceed the previous one. No one in Kentucky in this decade had the slightest justifiable reason for advocating the disruption of the Union. Quite to the contrary Kentucky had every reason for effecting compromises and making adjustments of sectional issues as they arose. They had everything to lose in a civil war.

This was the central motive which impelled several of Kentucky's sons to speak with such telling voices in the affairs of the Union. Almost to his death bed Henry Clay had pursued the cause of compromise of 1850; John Jordan Crittenden, James Guthrie, John Breckinridge, Abraham Lincoln, and Jefferson Davis were engaged in debating national issues in the Congress, or were influential in shaping national political views. Never before had Kentucky been so much a center of American political affairs, and never again would it muster so many strong voices in this area.

Despite the well-being of this age of the 1850's there were clouds on the Kentucky horizon. More and more the state's slave system came under public fire. In the opening of the 1850's Harriet Beecher Stowe had startled and angered many Kentuckians with her book *Uncle Tom's Cabin.*This publication brought both Kentucky slavery and morals under public scrutiny. Travelers, American and foreign, who visited the Ohio Valley in

UNCLE TOM'S CABIN;

OR,

LIFE AMONG THE LOWLY.

BY

HARRIET BEECHER STOWE.

VOL. I.

BOSTON:
JOHN P. JEWETT & COMPANY.
CLEVELAND, OHIO:
JEWETT, PROCTOR & WORTHINGTON.
1852.

the 1840's and 1850's drew insidious comparisons between progress made in the free states above the river, and that bound down by slavery south of it. Mrs. Stowe and the travelers were largely confirmed in their charges by advertisements which appeared in the Kentucky newspapers announcing the activities of slave traders. Handbills of the dealers were unsavory commentaries on Kentucky humanity, and so were the public auctions held on street corners where human beings were subjected to almost bestial indignities. This fact is eloquently reflected in entries in the Reverend William Pratt's diary for this period.

No Kentuckians in this era had a greater stake in peace and domestic harmony than those quiet and generous people, the Shakers of Pleasant Hill. They, like their worldly neighbors, despite cold, flood, and drouth, enjoyed prosperity in the pre-Civil War decade. By 1850 they had established a thriving trade in garden seeds, jellies and preserves, herbs, brooms, baskets, and woven goods down the river to the South. Their herds were among the finest in Kentucky. Elder Rufus Bryant proved himself not only an excellent herd manager, he was an astute trader and exhibitor. Wherever an auction of fine blooded stock occurred in central Kentucky, it was almost certain that Brother Rufus would be there running his experienced eye over the animals offered for sale. His Pleasant Hill herds of beef and dairy cattle became famous. His animals won ribbons in the local and state fairs. Indicative of Shaker interest in livestock was the entry in the general family journal for September 2, 1856, in which the community diarist noted, "Br. A. Ballance and J. R. Bryant went over to Woodford County to attend the Alexander's sale of fine stock and they returned on Thursday the 4th inst. having purchased two head of stock, one being for South Union".

The Shakers were a generous, peaceful, and religious people who remained neutral throughout four years of the Civil War.

From their bountiful supplies of food stored in the spacious cellars of the large Family Houses, they fed both armies as they passed through Pleasant Hill from time to time in the conquest for control of Central Kentucky.

All but one of the sick and wounded stragglers from the nearby Perryville battle field were nursed back to health. A Georgia boy died and was given a decent burial in the Shaker graveyard.

The ravages of War took its toll on the prosperous agricultural economy of Pleasant Hill starting a forty year decline which led to the dissolution of the Society in 1910.

At one time 492 Shakers lived in the Village.

9

The Meeting House—the scene of the religious dances of the Shakers (from a rare post-war photograph).

Large herds of cattle grazed the 4,000 acres of Shaker lands. Purebred Shorthorns were introduced to the area. Shaker herdsmen frequently were asked to judge fine cattle shows in Kentucky. (Photo—Joe Scheirich)

The Society carried on a thriving down river Southern trade. In a single year before the War, more than 79,000 papers of garden seeds, 17,000 jars of preserves and jellies, and 11,000 flat brooms were produced for sale.

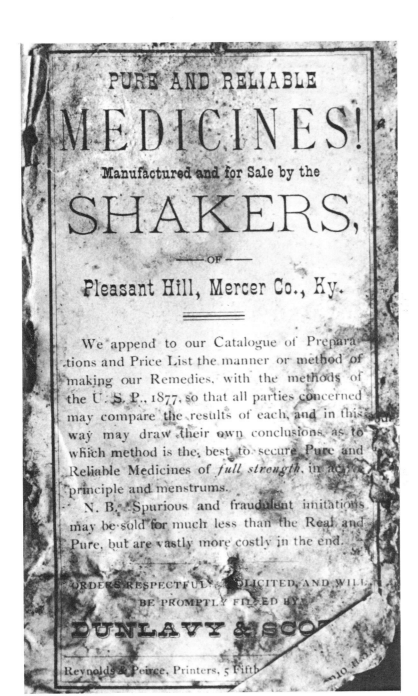

PURE AND RELIABLE

MEDICINES!

Manufactured and for Sale by the

SHAKERS,

—— OF ——

Pleasant Hill, Mercer Co., Ky.

We append to our Catalogue of Prepara-tions and Price List the manner or method of making our Remedies, with the methods of the U. S. P., 1877, so that all parties concerned may compare the results of each, and in this way may draw their own conclusions, as to which method is the best to secure Pure and Reliable Medicines of *full strength*, in active principle and menstrums.

N. B. Spurious and fraudulent imitations may be sold for much less than the Real and Pure, but are vastly more costly in the end.

ORDERS RESPECTFULLY SOLICITED, AND WILL BE PROMPTLY FILLED BY

DUNLAVY & SCOT

Reynolds & Peirce, Printers, 5 Fifth

In one bountiful year, the Shakers produced 3,000 pounds of medicinal herbs and made medicines for sale to the public. (Photo—James Ballard)

13

The Shakers were master builders

of brick and stone

and showed great skills in the crafts and in the architectural and mechanical arts.

A bench in the Pleasant Hill collection.

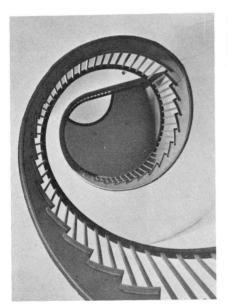

One of the twin spiral stairways which reach to a dome at the third floor of the Trustees House.

The Water House (left) with large tank on high stone pillars provided limestone spring water to all kitchens in the Family and Wash Houses as early
as 1833. Shoemaker's Shop (right). (Photo—Kalman Papp)

16

The miller at the grist mill which also served the surrounding farmers (from the rare photo collection).

While Shaker pastures yielded up hundreds of quality animals, their fields and gardens were equally as productive. They had, in 1850, either built or purchased modern cultivating and reaping machines. The result was the production of an abundance of corn and wheat to be ground at the Mill on the Kentucky for the southern river trade. The women and girls were equally as diligent in the gardens and kitchens growing, canning, and preserving fruits and vegetables. During this period the Shakers undertook to grow a type of oriental sorghum which they hoped would supply them with preserving sugars and syrups. Frequent were the entries in the Journal like the following for October 19, 1857, "L. Burnett and Geo. Stedman started to Maysville with garden seeds to sell", "October 17, 1859, M. Burnett and E. W. Scott started to New Orleans and that region trading", and "M. Burnett started to northern Illinois with cattle to sell, August 28, 1860."

Thus the Shaker world went about its daily chores. It brought orphan children into the Village, and saw "winter Shakers absconding when warm weather came". They invited a religious group of Swedes from Bishop Hill, Illinois, to join them, and these people came and went toward the closing years of the decade. The larger world of the "outside" faced turmoil over several national issues, principal of which was slavery. The Shakers had no militant policy against slavery, though they looked upon the institution with disfavor. Nevertheless they respected their neighbors' rights to own and dispose of slaves as they saw fit without engaging them in arguments. Occasionally they hired a slave from some nearby owner to perform farm work, or for an extended number of years. Sometimes converts brought slaves into the Society with the rest of their property. One such case was that of Jonah Crutcher who spent nineteen years at Pleasant Hill and was a convert. On January 4, 1859, the Society purchased him to prevent his sale south. Jonah had little time left to enjoy his new found freedom. He died on September 6, 1861, of dyspepsia. On August 28, 1860, Patsy Williamson Roberts died. She was brought to Pleasant Hill in 1807 as an eighteen year old slave by her owners. When they turned away from the Society they left Patsy behind to enjoy the freedom of the community.

By no means were the Shakers oblivious to the furious controversy raging over slavery. They were assiduous newspaper readers, and kept up with current events. Their salesmen who visited the Lower South became acutely aware of the threat to the Union itself. When James Buchanan asked the American people to observe a day of prayer on January 1, 1861, the Pleasant Hill Shakers obeyed the proclamation with the utmost sincerity. At heart they were fervent unionists, and the thought of dissolving the Union over slavery was too horrible for contemplation. In keeping with the presidential proclamation, the families at Pleasant Hill followed their regular routine of observing official and religious holidays. "We occupied the morning until half past 9, then gathered into our dwellings, and kept it a thanksgiving day. We had no union meeting at 10, [services] at 11, meeting at home at 1 P.M. We sang, and spoke, and prayed, etc., and closed." Until 4 P.M. that day this must have been one of the most ardent, and, perhaps, strangest responses in the Union.

There is no recorded evidence that the Shakers gave any serious notice to the presidential campaign the previous autumn. They knew, of course, of its outcome, and of the impulsive responses of the southern hotheads to its outcome. After February an interest close to home caught their undivided attention. They followed Kentucky's struggle to formulate a policy of armed neutrality. For the past fifty years the Shakers had faced another problem, and it was just now being solved. They wanted to open a good public road down the rocky face of the southern palisades of the Kentucky River to a suitable crossing place. Just as the national crisis was breaking they saw the road completed. On June 28, 1861, they held a day of jubilation to celebrate this important event. They prepared a sumptuous dinner and spread it under the trees along the new right-of-way for the Irish laborers who had chiseled the new road out of the rock face of the cliff. The road cost $12,000, and the Shakers paid for $7,000 of this bill.

Little did those jubilant people know in June, 1861, that almost immediately this road would become a veritable funnel through which military forces from both the Union and Confederate armies would flow. In fact it was less than fifteen months before endless lines of troops came that way, and less than a month before the first soldiers appeared in the main street of the village. One such company galloped into Pleasant Hill on August 1, 1861, and "mustered" in the street before the family houses. These early demonstrations by Confederate sympathizers were intended to harass the Shakers because of their antislavery and pacifist beliefs.

The Shaker Ferry at the Kentucky River. (From rare photo collection)

Chiseled out of the limestone Palisades in 1861, the new road to the River Landing became a short cut that funnelled soldiers from both armies into the Village above. (Photo—Joe Scheirich)

21

In 1861 a company of Confederate cavalry galloped into the Village and "mustered" on the road in front of the Family Houses.

CHAPTER II

"Devil with Devil Damned"

By early fall of the first year of the war the Shakers became well aware of the fact that the Nation was in for a long fight, and no doubt a holocaust. The sober old scribe who kept track of the world for the Society wrote, "The whole country is at present greatly agitated from one end to the other, on the question of Negro slavery, the North and the South being arranged against each other in deadly conflict. Some bloody battles have already been fought with various success; and the parties are training & drilling & trying to learn the most successful methods of letting out the heart's blood of their opponents, brother against brother, and father & son against each other. And for what! It is a doubtful question whether any of them on either side are able to tell what they are furiously seeking the lives of each other like demons for. It is certainly the most singular and sad spectacle that has ever been witnessed since the creation of the world—to see people possessing the best government ever vouched—safe by heaven to mortals on earth, commanding the admiration of the world—exhibiting unparalleled prosperity, peace & happiness, so far as freedom & the enjoyments of this world are concerned, a refuge for the oppressed of all nations, and the sacred rampart upon which was founded the hopes (now sadly changed to fears) of the pioneers in the principles of truth & liberty throughout the civilized world—and then to rise up without any cause, except disappointed ambition, rivalry & jealousy, and go to fighting like dogs, and butchering & murdering each other, and glorying in their deeds of blood like demons. And yet they claim to be good Christians, the true followers of the Prince of Peace, and appeal to the God of battles and pray for the success of their arms, on both sides, in slaying their brethren of their own church. And these are professed Christians! Lord what is man! Who is said to be possessed of a rational soul, and the noblest part of God's creation—and thus to be devouring each other, and that without cause; imbruing their hands in the fraternal blood, and then claiming a horrid reward for their satannical fratricide, in paltry gold & worldly glory. Truly did the immortal bard, reference to the fiends of hell, when he exclaimed: 'O shame to men! Devil with devil damned!' "

President Lincoln, like his predecessor James Buchanan, asked the American people to observe a day of humility, fasting, and prayer. The Shakers again were up by 4 A.M. on a rainy morning, September 26, 1861, and when they had finished their domestic chores they knelt in prayer in the several buildings and asked earnestly that God "would stay the hand of strife and roll back the flood of desolation that threatened the land—that he would dispose the hearts of the people & their rulers, as to cease their hostilities and restrain brethren from imbruing their hands in each other's blood—that they might sheath the sword, bury the rifle and cannon, and accept in lieu thereof the olive branch of peace, and let law and order, peace & happiness prevail throughout the land."

Nothing could have been more jarring to the Shakers than civil war. It threatened both their island of seclusion and their whole philosophy of human relationships. They realized that if war came there would be turned loose upon them the irreverent rowdies who would rob and pillage. Their attitude of resistance toward war would also involve them once again with a hostile public opinion. At Thanksgiving, 1861, the Shakers thanked God for blessings temporal and spiritual, but they realized that, "amidst the jarring elements of war & bloodshed that surround us; and prayed continuance of that protection & for the speedy termination of this unholy conflict."

Again at Christmas the village journalist reviewed the past year in which there was too much rain in the spring for the good of the fruit, a biting drouth cut the pasturage short, but there was a good crop of grain, and the community found itself comfortably well supplied with necessary food stuff. Only the great cloud of the "uncivil war" hovered over the Nation. It seemed to the diarist at Pleasant Hill unreasonable that, "in this most favored land, containing the best civil and political institutions that ever were known, since the world began," there should be war. "Yet with all this," he wrote, "the people have stirred up strife among themselves, the North and South arranged against each other, and are marshalling their embattled legions to a deadly conflict. And for what! All for nothing! The sceptre of power having passed from the South to the North, in the last presidential election, the former, under the plea of their cherished institution of slavery being endangered thereby, revolted, hence the present attitude of the belligerents."

The Shakers viewed the threatened war as a divisive conflict which reached every man and every home on the continent. Man they thought was in his last and fallen state, and that he no longer had the capacity to live happily and contented on this earth. Only a resurrection and a confrontation with his Maker could bring him lasting peace. This was truly a time of final testing with "Two immense armies, little less than a million, including both, such as the world never before witnessed, resting with one wing on the Atlantic Coast, Maryland, Virginia, Kentucky and Missouri into the vast prairies of Kansas, equipped with most efficient death-dealing implements that the ingenuity of man can produce are now facing each other with the grim visage of war, thirsting for blood, and threatening death and destruction, and slaughter with vengeance." This was indeed ill-becoming people in a nation which was then observing the birth of Christ in a holiday season.

While Pleasant Hill had the misfortune of being located on a main road north and south, the neighboring Shaker community of South Union, Kentucky, found itself enveloped within the newly formed Confederate lines which extended across southern Kentucky. On March 16, 1862, a letter from the South Union village was read in the church meeting at Pleasant Hill in which the author outlined for the central Kentucky congregation what would happen to it before the year's end by telling what was happening at South Union. A branch of the Federal Army had just delivered that village from the dominion of the Southern Confederacy. The South Union Shakers complained that the Confederates had pillaged and oppressed them. Secession troops had camped on the South Union premises, "and bands of marauders, plunderers and robbers thronged their streets & infested their premises, entering their barns, cribs and garners, and rifling them of their contents & spreading havoc and destruction in their course, and sometimes threatening to lay the beautiful village in ashes." A Federal invasion of Bowling Green drove the secessionists away, and the Union commander sent a band of cavalry to protect the village, "to the infinite joy of all the inhabitants." In this disturbing incident South Union was robbed of many of its horses, and it became necessary for the Believers at Pleasant Hill to replenish their neighbor's stock. On April 6, 1862, Brother Urban Johns was at Pleasant Hill to receive the horses.

LANDING OF OHIO TROOPS AT LOUISVILLE, KENTUCKY.—[SKETCHED BY MR. H. MOSLER.]

GENERAL BUELL'S ARMY ENTERING LOUISVILLE KENTUCKY.—DRAWN BY MR. H. MOSLER.—[SEE PAGE 653.]

28

THE WHARF AT LOUISVILLE—THE INHABITANTS LEAVING THE CITY.—Sketched by Mr. H. Mosler.—[See Page 654.]

Head-quarters of Gen¹. Buell, Louisville Ky.

CHAPTER III

The Grey Horde

Mid-summer, 1862, brought the war ever closer to Bluegrass Kentucky. On July 7, John Hunt Morgan led his command out of Livingston, Tennessee, headed for Tompkinsville in southern Kentucky. In the early morning of the 8th he was at Tompkinsville and began the mad dash into central Kentucky. At 9 A.M. Sunday morning, July 12th he was in Harrodsburg where he and his men found that the ladies had anticipated their coming and had prepared what Basil Duke called, "the most inviting rations." While the troopers gulped down a hearty breakfast, the men of Harrodsburg attended to the commands' horses. At Pleasant Hill the Shaker journalist noted on the next morning that, "Morgan (the Rebel) entered Harrodsburg, and the few Union troops that were there left and passed through here last night and today. They were hastening to reunite with the federal command in Lexington."

Although Morgan left Harrodsburg by way of the Lawrenceburg Pike and did not visit the Village, the Believers did not escape harassment. On September 3, 1862, Captain William C. P. Breckinridge appeared with a company of "John Morgan's guerilla band" on their way to Lexington to join the rest of the command and Kirby Smith's victorious troops in celebrating. It seemed to the isolated people of Pleasant Hill that now the Rebels were everywhere. Breckinridge's men stole two horses from the West Family, and if the Shakers had not acted in a hurry and hidden the rest of their animals, the Rebels no doubt would have taken them. Finding no more horses to steal, Breckinridge's men presented a pistol to Elder Rufus Bryant's head and threatened to take him to Lexington double quick if he did not reveal the place where the horses were hidden. Bryant refused their commands, and after searching the stables, lots, and pastures again without success they demanded food. The Shakers were now to get their first experience of running a military canteen. When at last Captain Billy's troops were in the saddle and galloping off down the hill to the river the scribe wrote, "A restless night ensued, watch being kept." The next day squads of southern sympathizers poured through the village hastening on to Lexington, "to rally under the standard of rebellion now raised in that city, and all night long the gathering continued."

Two days later, on September 6th, about a hundred of Morgan's followers appeared at Pleasant Hill coming back from Lexington on their way to Harrodsburg. This hungry horde stopped off for supper and was fed. They camped for the night in the Office Stable Lot, and threw out pickets on all the roads and approaches. Now war had become a very real thing for the Shakers, and they bedded down for the night with its minions surrounding them. "We were completely hemmed in," said the journalist, "and guarded by the Southern Confederacy." All this activity presented a threat in another quarter. The Shaker youth became restive and some of them wanted to join the armed forces. Thomas Chaplin accidentally shot himself in the foot as he prepared to join the Rebels. This first contingent of Confederates moving to the southwest, unlike those under Breckinridge's command, behaved civilly and respectfully and after breakfast moved on toward Harrodsburg without trying to ransack stable and pasture.

"MORGAN'S MEN" HERE

Shakers hid their horses as CSA Gen. J. H. Morgan's cavalry came this way July 13, 1862. But he forbade command to trespass or molest Shakers out of respect for their religion. Grateful for this good treatment Shakers fed Morgan and his men magnificently as they retreated through here on Oct. 11, 1862 after Battle of Perryville. See map on other side.

1963   KENTUCKY HISTORICAL SOCIETY   KENTUCKY DEPARTMENT OF HIGHWAYS   627

From July 1, 1862, until the end of the war Pleasant Hill was not again to experience freedom from anxiety and fright caused by troop movements and guerilla raids. Almost every day after September 1st there was fresh excitement. On the 6th, 7th, and 8th secession troops were present in the village by the thousands asking to be fed and watered. The wells were low, and the new crop was still in the fields. Horses and cattle had to be kept well hidden and guarded day and night, even so, "Marauders parade the streets demanding them, & traverse the pastures & fields in search of them."

Rumors were numerous. Every soldier had a tale to tell, and excited neighbors rushed in with stories of impending calamity, all of which the Shakers could believe. In their isolation, and now surrounded by troops, they could not determine what was happening or where it was going to happen. They feared there would be a pitched battle in their streets. The thing that made the situation was that troops marched and counter-marched through the village. Where were they going, and what was the meaning of their frantic rushing around?

In the midst of all this movement life for the Shakers was now completely disrupted. Every time a new contingent of troops passed through Pleasant Hill they stopped and ate with the Believers, and every new gathering offered that much greater threat to property and hidden livestock. The pastures were dotted with prowling marauders. Unknown to the Shakers these were the days when the indecisive Braxton Bragg was trying to place Richard Hawes in the Governor's chair in Frankfort, and at the same time was attempting to keep his rear covered against a surprise attack by Don Carlos Buell. If all this frantic marching and counter-marching made no sense to the Shakers, it seemed more idiotic to Kirby Smith, John Hunt Morgan, and Colonel John Wharton.

In a critical note on Bragg, Basil Duke said there were about 56,000 Confederates in Kentucky in the latter part of September. These were strung out from Bardstown to Frankfort and Lexington, and from Lawrenceburg to Bryantsville and Camp Dick Robinson. Duke said the bulk of Bragg's army had marched from Bardstown and Springfield to get in the rear of Buell's forces. Five or six thousand Federal troops under Dumont were sent to Frankfort to break up the inauguration. Of the fiasco at the statehouse Captain Duke observed that Bragg "made one of the first and best men in the state, a man of venerable years and character, held in the universal respect for his kind, open, manly nature, and especially honored by the Southern people of Kentucky for his devotion to the cause—General Bragg made this old man, who had been unanimously indicated as the proper man for provisional governor of Kentucky, tell the people who crowded to listen to his inaugural address, that the state would be held by the Confederate Army, cost what it might." At the very time that General Bragg so deceived Governor Hawes, and made him unwillingly deceive his people, the Confederate Army had already commenced to retreat.

A miscalculation as to where General Kirby Smith's forces would meet the Federals caused an immediate necessity to shift forces from a position between Versailles and Frankfort to Lawrenceburg. Thus it was that Pleasant Hill was caught almost in the very eye of all this reshuffling of troops. On one of the passes through Pleasant Hill the Confederates commandeered seven two-horse wagons loaded with supplies and made the Shakers drive them to Lexington. Micajah Burnett, William Runyan, and B. Byrum went with the wagons on the promise that they would be paid for the property. They were—in southern scrip which the journalist branded "worthless trash." He had more to say, "This is southern rights,

"Worthless trash" to the Shakers.

36

liberty and freedom from oppression is it? Well that is enough of such deliverance." The old scribe had no doubt read John Hunt Morgan's famous horseback orations on deliverance. The brethren who went to Lexington returned late at night, wending their way out and in among troops with one of the West Family's wagons and $640 in Confederate bills.

Before the returning wagoneers could report on what they had seen on the road to Lexington, news came that 15,000 Confederate troops had gathered in Harrodsburg, and that war with its grim cannon-mouth horrors was leaping madly toward the heart of the Pleasant Hill Zion itself.

So frantic were the closing days of September and the first week of October that the journalist who had always kept a meticulous account of the weather had little time to say more than there was a galling drouth. Sources of water supply for the village and farms were daily being exhausted. As the diarist said, "the pastures are parched and the water fountains so dried up, that the stock are much pinched for food and drink. The tanyard spring yields 2 gallons per minute." The ground in the fields was too parched and hard to plow, grapes and late fruits were maturing poorly, and there was the grim necessity to feed a precious stock of winter hay to the cattle.

By October 3rd the Shakers were so beset by problems created by the war that they could give almost no attention to everyday affairs of the village. The scribe did note that James Passley and Richard Staples had absconded from the East House, and as usual he threw his inky condemnation after them as worthless bits of trash. Maybe unfortunately the fleeing trash was caught and returned to their house.

Far more ominous than absconding boys was the fact that neighbors' wagons loaded with produce were being driven through the village on the way to Lexington to satisfy further Braxton Bragg's insatiable desire for stores. On the 6th General Humphrey Marshall's brigade of Confederates entered the village with its endless wagon train. This command pulled into the North Pond lot and camped—in fact Marshall's night camp was strung out along the road to beyond the Kentucky River. Confederate forces were now converging on Perryville over the new road leading up from the Kentucky River, and the one in which the Shakers took so much pride, was now an open funnel feeding the war into Pleasant Hill.

So it was the marching grey hordes poured through the Shaker village and the Believers got a close-up view of the Confederate Army. The troops who came with Marshall's command were fairly well-clothed and supplied. Behind them, however, came a ragged, greasy, dirty, and barefoot band who "looked more like the bipeds of pandemonium, than the beings of this earth or the angels of deliverance from Lincoln's bondage."

Like the endless phalanxes of a biblical exodus the weary wavering line of Confederates suffering from heat, want of water, and dust, "marched into our yards & surrounded our wells like the locusts of Egypt," said the Shaker journalist, "and struggled with each other for the water as if perishing with thirst, and they thronged our kitchen doors and windows, begging for bread like hungry wolves, we nearly emptied our kitchens of their contents, and they tore the loaves and pies into fragments, and devoured them as eagerly as if they were starving. Some even threatened to shoot others if they did not divide with them."

Pleasant Hill stores of foodstuffs were all but exhausted, and it became necessary to drive the beggars from the wells and kitchen doors. The Shakers did not dare ring their bells to indicate the various meal periods

The New Road to the Landing, once the pride of the Shakers, was torn to pieces by the tramping of thousands of cavalry and heavy ordnance wagons. (Photo—Joe Scheirich)

39

of the day for fear of bringing a bounding mob up to the doors crying for food and drink. The brethren and sisters were exhausted from long hours before stoves, or working in bins and pantries preparing meals.

In spite of shoving and fussing among the troops they offered no real violence to the Shakers themselves. There was even a distinct show of gratefulness for kindnesses. Many soldiers pressed their hosts to accept pay, but the Shakers refused compensation even though they exhausted their precious winter's supply of food feeding literally thousands of soldiers.

Late in the afternoon of October 6, Colonel Abraham Buford's command of 600 mounted men arrived in Pleasant Hill, and almost in the middle of the village received orders to return to Lexington. This reverse order caused the Shaker observer to write, "The wave recoiled and crowded like the rushing of waters." Ordnance wagons were driven into the East Family lot to turn around. Cannon and other arms were all but brushed against the walls of the dwelling, a sight of horror to the bystanders. That night the Shakers bedded down amidst an armed camp of sleeping soldiers and their infernal machines of destruction and blood letting.

Fortunately Buford's camping troops committed little trespass. They burned a few panels of rail fence, and made off with some hay and sweet potatoes, otherwise they respected the property of their unwilling hosts. All day on the 7th there was an endless procession of troops hastening toward Harrodsburg. Just as on the day before the Shakers cooked and fed the ravenous mob throughout the day and until after midnight when the sisters were too exhausted to do further work. The next day their old friend General Kirby Smith's supply wagons rumbled back through the village headed for Lexington—another reverse movement.

Soldiers camped on the Village campus. At times ordnance wagons and mounted men were a scene of horror to the peaceful Shakers. (Photo—Joe Scheirich)

All day on October 8, 1862, the sisters were again in the kitchens cooking and baking, and the brethren were feeding the troops. This time the sounds of war welled up from the southwest. Off toward Danville, Perryville, and Harrodsburg the thunder of cannon and the roar of battle sounded like the doom of Armageddon. The village diarist could only exclaim, "Lamentable, to reflect, that human beings would slaughter and butcher each other, and then claim to be the image and offsprings of God who is loved." Every roar of a gun in this battle did indeed tear the images of God asunder. Little could the old Shaker journalist visualize that within fifteen or twenty air-line miles blood ran like water on that hot cheerless October day in one of the fiercest fights in the war.

For Pleasant Hill the Miltonian drama was endless. There were troops in the carpenter shop, the roads were crowded, as were the family lots, and the incessant clump of feet and clatter of wagon and boom of cannon had now become synchronized with eternity itself. Zion had turned into an island of depravity, and rumors of every sort were afloat. Soldiers passed on army gossip, frightened neighbors rushed in with fresh tales of horror and the Shakers added their own imaginings. Colonel Jackson Allen rushed up with a fresh detachment of Kirby Smith's ravening wolves and camped in the West Pond Lot, while the main body of General Smith's command was harbored in the North Pond Lot. For the Shakers the 9th of October was a bone-crushing day of labor followed by another frantic night of watching for an evil that would roll out of darkness to engulf at last their beloved haven. A false alarm in the night caused Jack Allen's troops to skedaddle, and left the Shakers trying to guess what impending menace would threaten them the next moment.

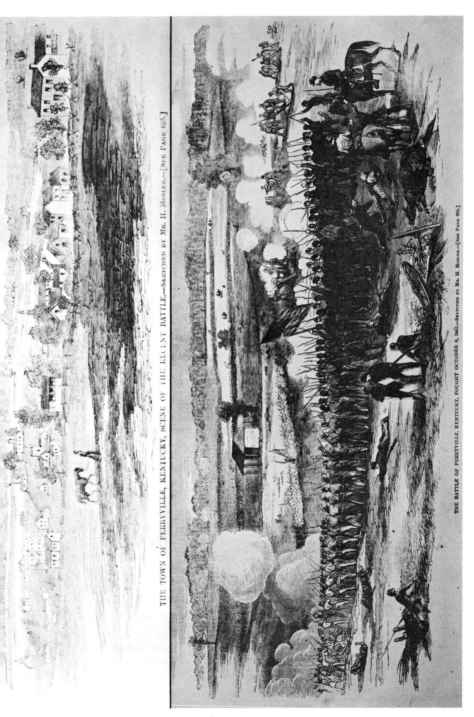

THE TOWN OF PERRYVILLE, KENTUCKY, SCENE OF THE RECENT BATTLE.—Sketched by Mr. H. Mosler.—[See Page 695.]

THE BATTLE OF PERRYVILLE, KENTUCKY, FOUGHT OCTOBER 8, 1862.—Sketched by Mr. H. Mosler.—[See Page 695.]

43

DOMESTIC INTELLIGENCE.

THE BATTLE OF PERRYVILLE.

The following is official :

PERRYVILLE, KENTUCKY, October 9.
VIA BARDSTOWN, Oct 10, 1862.

To Major-General Halleck, General-in-Chief :

I have already advised you of the movements of the army under my command from Louisville. More or less skirmishing has occurred daily with the enemy's cavalry. Since then it was supposed the enemy would give battle at Bardstown. My troops reached that point on the 4th inst , driving out the enemy's rear-guard of cavalry and artillery. The main body retired toward Springfield, whither the pursuit was continued. The centre corps, under General Gilbert, moved on the direct road from Springfield to Perryville, and arrived on the 7th inst. within two miles of the town, where the enemy was found to be in force. The left column, under General M'Cook, came upon the Naxville road about ten o'clock yesterday (the 8th inst.). It was ordered into position to attack, and a strong reconnoissance directed. At four o'clock I received a request from General M'Cook for reinforcements, and learned that the left had been severely engaged for several hours, and that the right and left of that corps were being turned and severely pressed. Reinforcements were immediately sent forward from the centre. Orders were also sent to the right column, under General Crittenden, which was advancing by the Lebanon road, to push forward and attack the enemy's left ; but it was impossible for it to get in position in time to produce any decisive result. The action continued until dark. Some fighting also occurred on the centre *The enemy were every where repulsed,* but not without some momentary advantage on the left. The several corps were put in position during the night, and moved to the attack at six o'clock this morning. Some skirmishing occurred with the enemy's rear-guard. The main body had fallen back in the direction of Harrodsburg. I have no accurate report of our loss yet. It is probably retty heavy, including valuable officers. Generals Jackson and Terril. I regret to say, are among the killed.   D. C. BUELL,
                         Major-General Commanding.

ANOTHER VICTORY.

Another brilliant victory in Kentucky was reported on 12th. Dispatches received from Lebanon state that there was a great battle fought on Saturday 11th, between Harrodsburg and Danville, heavier and more severe than that of 8th at Perryville. Colonel Woolford, of the Kentucky Union cavalry, captured one hundred and sixty wagons and a thousand prisoners. The rebels, at last accounts, were retreating to Camp Dick Robinson.

44

October 10th brought no surcease from the horrible war. Confederate regulars pushed on to Harrodsburg while camp stragglers, guards and other marauders halted in the village to beg food and exhaust the meager water supply. Now the recorder noted, "We are feeding hundreds daily, and have fed thousands this week. They plead hunger, thirst, sickness, fatigue, and privations till charity and sympathy are irresistibly awakened in their behalf, and we supply them with such as we can afford. The distant sound of cannon again today [Oct. 10] a little west of south, announces that they are belching forth death and destruction into the ranks of the belligerents."

There was a recoil from the battle lines. The tug of war had risen and waned, now came the Confederates falling back in retreat. Hosts of soldiers were back at the doors of their hospitable benefactors more ravenous than ever. Several hundred of the vanguard of the retreating army camped during the night of the 10th in Dr. Campbell's pasture and were foraging in the Shaker's cornfield. This wanton act threatened hardship for the villagers who were then at the point of physical exhaustion. Feelingly the journalist lamented, "We cannot help ourselves. To make a charge, we receive trash like leaves, and to refuse it we lay ourselves liable to arrest and punishment. And there is danger in arousing the lion of secessia, which would be like carrying firebrands over a magazine that is under our feet. Ho for Southern Rights! Liberty! and Freedom!"

In Harrodsburg a hardhanded son of southern liberty had snatched Brother Rufus Bryant's horse away from him on the streets. General Bragg promised to have the horse returned, but it could not be found. "More southern rights with a witness, one company came and paid 30 dollars in southern scrip for their part. Such a day as this has never been witnessed on Pleasant Hill before, and God grant that it may never again." Such was October

10, 1862. The only evidence that the Shakers could discern that God still existed was the fact that three quarters of an inch of rain laid the dust and stirred the mud. The water supply was partially restored, but troopers at the well drank the water as fast as it collected.

Where dust had stifled the villagers for ten days, now the clomping feet of rebel soldiers dragged the land up to the doors of the dwellings in the form of mud. The arrival of more than a thousand wagons in Bragg's famous supply train accompanied by guards and attendants moving on toward Lexington tore to pieces the new road down to the river. Behind this lumbering train came Colonel Abe Buford's cavalry, and behind them could be heard the ever-tightening ring of cannon fire on the road between Danville and Harrodsburg, and only eight or ten air-line miles away. "O God! Protect this heritage from the ravages of cruel war," prayed a desperate elder. On and on went the badgering cries for food and water. A temporary table was mounted across the front lawn of the Office, and was kept filled all day. More than a thousand battle stained soldiers ate at this table and shambled off greasy mouthed toward the river. "And yet they beg food and clothing, and almost everything used for the comfort of life. They offer to purchase everything they call for, but we have uniformly declined any compensation for these things and they are lavish with their thanks for our hospitality." The theme of daily entries in the village journal had come to have a monotony, soldiers, work, begging, exhaustion, and the roar of war.

Late in the afternoon of October 11 there appeared in Pleasant Hill one of the most dramatic scenes in Kentucky military history. It developed as quickly as if it had been flashed on a giant screen, and had full resemblance to the movement of giant armies of Athenians and Trojans. The Village roads filled in every direction

As 10,000 hungry Confederate troops passed through from the Battle of
Perryville, tables were set up along the road in front of the Trustees House.
After feeding 1,400, the food cellars of the Shakers were almost empty.

with cavalry bounding headlong from Harrodsburg, Lawrenceburg, and Danville. As far as the eye could see there were horsemen. The Shakers believed the column pitching down upon them from the southwest was Forrest's command—it was perhaps that of Kirby Smith.

Instantly, there appeared in the South Lane what seemed to be the endless ranks of John Hunt Morgan's cavalry, as the Shaker journalist labeled it, "the celebrated guerilla chief John Morgan's command" and it contained approximately 1800 men. Up from the east came General John Wharton's column. "Thus we were invaded," said the Elder, "from every public avenue to the village except the one north toward Lexington, in this the dark mass filed away in haste and soon disappeared. General Morgan informed us that he and his command had intended taking up lodging with us, but that our generosity had induced him to move farther to avoid oppressing us. Two of the company attempted to press a horse a piece, but counter orders from the General prevented it."

Morgan was in a highly agitated mood that day. He had been ordered by Bragg on October 10 to take up a position six miles from Harrodsburg on the Danville Pike. He reconnoitered the Danville-Harrodsburg front all that night. Before him was a small unit of Federal cavalry and an infantry regiment which he had charged early in the morning of the 11th, but about one or two P.M. he learned that Bragg was retreating toward Bryantsville, and with the enemy on three sides Morgan decided to fall back. Thus it was that he appeared in Pleasant Hill late in the afternoon. Duke in later years confirmed the Shaker journalist in his timing and descriptions of troop movements. He further confirmed the Shaker statements when he wrote his memoirs four years later. "Colonel Morgan," he said, "had always respected

In the South Lane appeared 1,800 of Morgan's Cavalry. From the east came Wharton's columns, "Thus we were invaded from every public avenue." (Photo by Linda Hockensmith)

the peaceful and hospitable 'Shakers,' and had afforded them, whenever it became necessary, protection, strictly forbidding all members of his command to trespass upon them in any way. We were consequently great favorites in the Village, and on this occasion derived great benefits from the perfect rectitude of conduct which we had always observed—'in that part of the country.' The entire community resolved itself into a culinary committee, and cooked the most magnificent meal for the command. It was with deep regret we tore ourselves away on the next morning."

MORGAN HOUSE

HOME OF JOHN HUNT MORGAN
"THUNDERBOLT OF THE CONFEDERACY"
BORN HUNTSVILLE, ALA. 6-1-1825
KILLED GREENEVILLE, TENN. 9-4-1864
LIEUTENANT - KENTUCKY VOLUNTEERS
IN MEXICAN WAR 1846-1847 MAJOR
GENERAL - C. S. A., 1861-1864.
—HISTORICAL MARKERS SOCIETY—

At Second and Mill Streets in Lexington. Also was home of Thomas Hunt Morgan, Kentucky's only Nobel Scholar. Now a Museum owned by Bluegrass Trust for Historic Preservation.

CHAPTER IV

The Thunder of Mars in Zion

On the night of the 11th Pleasant Hill experienced its first lull in the storm of war. The West Lot had two horses stolen, but the muddy main road was at last quiet after eight or ten thousand cavalrymen had ridden on, and the last heavy-footed infantryman had dragged himself around the bend going north. "The rising moon shed a silvery light over this Pleasant Hill of Zion, as soft and placid as Milton's night in the Paradise of our first parents."

The Miltonian spell was quickly broken. If the sisters that night dreamed of a Shaker heaven where there were no more soldiers, the early morning bell quickly called them back to a world of reality. Before the sun had come above the wide Bluegrass Plateau the stragglers from Perryville began to appear. A part of Gano's and Morgan's command returned for breakfast, "Which was produced with alacrity, and they came in from the Lexington Road where they were encamped, and occupied our streets, and the captains marched their companions into the Office Yard by turns and made them sit down upon the ground, and with the help of the brethren served out their rations, which occupied two hours or more. During this time the sisters were cooking and baking with all the means at their command to keep a supply, till about 400 had eaten."

When these troopers had eaten they rode out the Lexington Road and formed a battle line to protect the rear of the retreating soldiers. Again the journalist was forced to view his beloved Zion through the bloodshot eyes of war. "How awful," he wrote, "to think of a wicked and bloody battle occurring in the midst of Zion on earth! Those [soldiers] in the village placed a strong guard at the crossroads, by the carpenter's shop, and occupied the road back to the North Family, and picket guards and couriers patrolled the streets and road toward Harrodsburg until one o'clock P.M. when General Morgan ordered them to move up the road a piece, and not disturb the tranquility of our people any longer. General Morgan and his staff came up and took dinner and returned again towards the river."

Scarcely had Morgan and his men disappeared before Confederates were rushing headlong through Pleasant Hill from the southwest. Rumor was afloat that immediately in their rear a force of 30,000 Federal Troops were pressing northward toward Lexington. Fortunately this scare was without substance, and not many troops actually reached the village. Nevertheless cannon boomed and men marched all day Sunday. Happily for the Shakers all the movement of troops in and around Pleasant Hill resulted in no appreciable depredations. Except for some rapscallions trying to steal a couple of horses, Morgan and his men had set an example of politeness and this tended to curb the aggressiveness of other troops.

As the Confederates retreated they formed a semicircle north and east of the village. A circle of campfires burned brightly all across the horizon in these directions. Fires could be spotted as far away as Camp Dick Robinson, Bryantsville, and the high banks of the Kentucky River. In the village itself there was an eerie calmness. Out on those far-flung ridges were literally thousands of soldiers, and large numbers of them might not live to see another sunset if all the rumors were true. To the southwest and south there was a rim of darkness, and no one ventured a guess as to what terror would stumble out of this quarter before daybreak.

"Strange events," said the recorder. "Who ever would have thought that this secluded and sacred spot of truly Pleasant Hill, would ever have been surrounded by embattled legions, within hearing distance in almost every direction from this point; and the warring hosts traversing our streets and premises to and fro day and night, with their weapons of death, guns, swords, and bayonets gleaming in the sun, with the rebel banner flying, the cannon trundling over the pavements, and even through our yards, going to meet the enemy, and while yet in sounding distance, belching forth slaughter and carnage into their ranks! Where the clash of arms and din of war proclaims the raging thirst for blood, power and glory, that fills the ambitions (alas inhuman) breast! And yet that we should have escaped with comparatively little damage, clearly implies, that whatever of evil may be among us, (and God knows there is enough) there is still a spark of light, a remnant of faith, a seed of truth, and a righteous few in the heritage of God, which He holds in the hollow of His hand, and has preserved as the precious jewels of His choice; while the contending armies have laid waste the country around, and desolation marks their course of blood throughout the land, 'I will sing unto thee Lord as long as I live; I will sing praise to my God while I have my being.'"

This earnest supplication was followed with an answer. The morning of October 13th failed to bring the holocaust which both rumor and Shaker had predicted would happen. Instead Bragg's army was moving southward through Nicholasville and Camp Dick Robinson. After a few days' visit in Lexington, Morgan and his men turned back toward their favorite raiding territory, that along the Louisville and Nashville Railroad. On the 29th of

October they were in Hopkinsville enjoying a full show of hospitality from the people of that city. Buell's troops still boomed a few cannon shots, but the fire of war was now gone out at Perryville and in the Bluegrass. Only roving bands of stragglers now concerned the Shakers. These cut-throats from both armies, or more particularly, from neither army, were beasts of "pealth and stealth." A twenty-five year old horse was stolen from the mill. The sneak-thieves caused the Believers to keep an ever closer watch on their livestock. "But of all Rebel officers that have visited us," said the village diarist, "not one has shown the least disposition to molest us, except Captain Breckinridge, son of the Reverend Robert J. Breckinridge (as true a patriot as walks on American soil) with his vandal horde of Kentuckians, and one who pressed the wagons." There is more than a suggestion here that Breckinridge's men were also guerillas.

What relief it was for the people of Pleasant Hill to learn on the morning of the 14th that the Rebels were finally on the run toward the South. The night before the fires had flickered and gone out around the rim of the plateau. In the distance a booming of Buell's cannon had moved off to the outer perimeter about Crab Orchard and Stanford. Once again the routine of village life could be resumed. Horses, wagons, cloth, flour and preserves could now be returned to their proper places.

There was however, an occasional pitiful straggler who came to Pleasant Hill from the Perryville battlefield. One of these was William Henry Centlaw, a parolee from Georgia who was left behind by the retreating Confederates. Early in the morning of October 24th he died, and that afternoon three Shaker elders bore his crude home-made casket to the humble Believers' cemetery, and there beside the graves of the faithful they deposited his body. Charitable members of the community gave their services

The Shaker Graveyard. Initials only appear on headstones. Here was buried the Confederate boy from Georgia. (Photo—Joe Scheirich)

and medical supplies to the treatment of the wounded in Danville and Harrodsburg, just as they had been hospitable to the troops before their kitchen doors.

Not until November 15th was the main road through the village to hear again the martial thunder of troops on the move. This time the 95th Illinois under the command of Colonel Champion passed that way with colors flying, and eight fifers and five drummers playing Yankee Doodle. Unlike the Rebels who plagued the faithful in early October, these troops were well-clothed, and presented a snappy appearance. What was even more attractive about them they were under good discipline and were civil and orderly. Too, they were well fed.

A serious problem confronted all the Shakers in the United States. A letter was read at Pleasant Hill on November 16th in public meeting which described the distress of the New Lebanon, N. Y., community. A Shaker by the name of George Ingalls had been drafted into the Army of the United States. Benjamin Gates, a trustee of the village, called on President Lincoln concerning this act and obtained a reprieve for Ingalls.

Promises were made that in the future a petition of affirmation should be drawn before the proper authorities and members of the Society would be exempted from military service. The Shakers had in their history considerable experience with public oppression in this area dating back to the War of 1812.

CHAPTER V
Wolves in the Fold

In his entry closing out the year of 1862 the scribe
looked back over the past twelve months of trouble. The
growing season had not been an unusually favorable one.
Crops were short by a third of potential production, ap-
ples had failed to mature properly, and there was hardly
a half crop of broom corn and potatoes. The marvel was
that the Shakers had anything left. The journalist con-
cluded, "But the most important events have transpired
in the political and military world, that ever occurred on
this continent, or perhaps any other, since the world began, or since the expulsion of the Arch Fiend from the
Empyrean of Jehovah. That most unholy and fraticidal
war which has been waged in this disturbed century, has
raged with the fury of the Beast, and with capricious fortune, and has hurled its thousands into the dark abyss
below. It has emphatically been the year of battles and
human slaughter." In a more direct way the year ended
in disaster for the Shakers when fifty Federal cavalrymen
dashed out of Harrodsburg and sank the ferries and boats
on the Kentucky River about the Shaker Landing to prevent their being used by John Hunt Morgan who was
then in the Green River country, and rumor had it that
he was headed once again for the Bluegrass. Not all was
lost, however, because some of the Pleasant Hill boats
were hustled downriver to Frankfort and safety.

Late in March, 1863, L. Burnett rushed home from a
trading visit to Springfield to report that rumors were
rampant that the Confederates were in that country. At
least a thousand soldiers had reached Danville, and Fed-

RECEPTION OF THE NINTH INDIANA VOLUNTEERS AT DANVILLE, KENTUCKY, AFTER DRIVING OUT THE REBELS.—Drawn by Mr. H. Mosler.—[See Page 715.]

eral troops were said to be flying before them. Near panic seized the countryside. Stage coaches were driven away from Harrodsburg and neighboring towns and villages around midnight. Livestock was hastened to cover once again, and all sorts of goods were hustled out of sight. Again the river was swept clear of boats by the Federal troops, and the mail ceased to run. The Shaker journalist said, "The atmosphere floated with rumors as plenty as leaves in autumn, and a general commotion prevails." Once again there was the thunder of cannon, and war crept closer to Pleasant Hill for a second time. News came that General Ambrose Burnside had arrived in Cincinnati with a strong force on his way to central Kentucky. This allayed the panic. The Shakers returned to sawing wood with their new circular saw, but they took pains to post a sentinel in Harrodsburg so as not to be caught by surprise. On March 23, he informed the villagers that the Rebels were gone; they had left Harrodsburg at midnight, "carrying away all the horses, mules, and cattle they could collect south of here, and are flying back to Tennessee & burnt two turnpike bridges on Dix River to prevent pursuit."

For the next two years of the war life went on in Pleasant Hill at a fairly even and undisturbed pace, except for occasional visits from those unearthly scoundrels, the thieving and murderous Kentucky guerillas. There were no further organized military invasions. Being at heart loyal unionists, the Believers observed all the public prayer and fast days proclaimed by the Governor of Kentucky and President Lincoln.

Life was not without its disturbances. Rumors continued to reach the Shakers that the Rebels would return to Kentucky. A panic broke out once again in Harrodsburg when a company of Rebels entered the town on July 5th and 6th, 1863. Once again livestock and goods were sent into hiding. A little after midnight of the 10th a squad of Federal troops entered Pleasant Hill and began a search for rebel troops which they believed were sheltered there. The Shakers had to feed these invaders and their horses. On June 10, 1864, the mail stage returned from Nicholasville with news that it could not reach Lexington because John Hunt Morgan had driven the Union forces away, and now controlled the town. "Here we are again shut up from the outer world, without any mails, and every breeze that stirs is freighted with conflicting rumors from the invaders, who are reported on all sides of us & apprehensions are entertained that booty and plunder may attract their cupidity to our peaceful borders."

This appeared to be what was happening on the morning of July 11th when crashing artillery fire awakened the villagers. This attack was made by raiders coming from Frankfort, but the Rebels were repulsed before they reached Pleasant Hill. "Painful anxiety & combat vigilance day & night, are the attendants of our present isolated and constant and imperiled situation, by reason of this rebel raid."

By 1864, the guerilla menace had reached serious proportions, as bands of marauders, primarily stragglers and deserters, roamed over the countryside, not so much bent on harrying the enemy, as on "stealth and destruction." The Shakers expressed apprehension that "booty and plunder may attract their cupidity to our peaceful borders." On the night of October 7th, the Shaker premonitions were fulfilled when an armed banditti, led by Captain Sam Berry, formerly of Morgan's command and who, as a youth was reared at Pleasant Hill, attacked the mail stage on the bridge over Shawnee Run by the mill dam. The guerillas, after robbing the stage and rifling the mail sacks, held up all "who happened to be passing dur-

At the bridge over Shaker Creek, guerillas held up the stage, robbed the passing Shakers of watches and money and held up other passers-by for two hours. The original was a covered bridge built before 1848.

ing their stay," a period of two hours. Unfortunately, El-hanon W. Scott, Henry Daily and a few sisters were then returning from Harrodsburg. Scott was relieved of his watch and $3, and though forced to hand over $27, the quick-thinking Daily slipped a couple of watches and $3 to the sisters who secreted them. More serious was the loss of two fine Shaker horses, with which the bandits escaped, as they rode on to Harrodsburg, robbing the toll gate as they went. The Believers estimated their loss at $150, yet "a fortunate escape under such a fiendish raid."

There was reason enough for the Shakers to feel anxiety when sometime later nine Confederate troops rode up from the Shaker ferry about four o'clock in the afternoon and made a dash for the horse lots. The breth-ren and sisters rushed out to meet them, but to their great relief the Rebels jumped their horses over the fences and rode off across the pastures. That night the Believers hid most of their horses, and kept wakeful vigil over the vil-lage itself.

It was a relief on June 22nd to see a company of Fed-eral troops ride westward. This was a certain sign that Re-bels and guerillas were swept back once again. It was not until September 28th that Pleasant Hill experienced an-other disturbance. This time a band of about twenty guerillas came searching the lots and pastures for horses. They were driven from the center horse lot by The-ophilus, the Negro blacksmith, and his dog. The thieves succeeded only in leading away a two year old colt worth $180.

The Shakers either did not know of the surrender of General Lee or took no notice of it. On April 14, 1865, however, the journalist made an antedated entry of the assassination of Abraham Lincoln, and the attempt made on the life of William S. Seward. It was with righteous anger that the recorder wrote, "Just at this juncture when a four years bloody conflict, which was inaugurated by the most deeply plotted, extensive and wicked rebellion that has ever been witnessed since the world began, was approachirg a favorable termination, by the crushing of the rebellion, & the restoration of the Union, & of peace to the country, the evil genius of this dark fiendish rebellion has given to the wide world an exhibition of the venom that rankled in the heart of the nation in the diabolical assassination of its chief magistrate."

Lee may have surrendered at Appomattox, and Joe Johnson had acceded to General W. T. Sherman's demands at the Bennett House in North Carolina, but for the Shakers at Pleasant Hill there were to be other unhappy incidents growing out of the war. On the night of April 25th, 1865, a band of six mounted and heavily armed highwaymen rode into the village, broke into the postoffice by using blocks of stone taken from the front steps, capsized the letter press, and with a piece of iron mauled from the stove smashed in the other doors of the building and rifled through the contents of the office without finding much money.

These ruffians then searched every apartment in the Office building, and the leader ordered his companions to take Brother Rufus Bryant dead or alive with the hope that he could be made to bring out the Shaker funds. Bryant escaped by a back door, leaving Micajah Burnett and three sisters to confront the robbers. Brother Rufus aroused the whole village and quickly sentinels appeared on the scene. The guerillas fired wildly into the crowd but hit no one. They threatened to kill several of the brethren, but by the time the alarm bell on top of the Center Family House had been rung and the whole population of the village was astir, the fiends retreated.

As the bandits rushed to their horses they fired a volley of shots back at the buildings. One ball broke a side glass

A band of 6 guerillas broke into the post office (first left) and ransacked the Trustees Office next door while Brother Rufus Bryant escaped from the rear to crawl around the Meeting House . . .

to ring the bell on top of the Center Family House. Aroused from their
sleep, the Shakers swept into the road and frightened the robbers . . .

who mounted and shot through the front door of the Trustees House and . . .

then rode through the Village, shooting into buildings as they took off toward Harrodsburg . . .

one bullet went through the door of the West Family House and landed in the dining room as Dr. Pennebaker was coming down the stairs. (Series of photos by Joe Scheirich)

of the Trustees Office and went through the sash of the door at the far end of the hall, glancing off the ceiling and penetrating the dining room door at the end of the porch. One struck the Meeting House, another perforated the front door of the West Family House and went into the dining room just as William Pennebaker was coming down the front stairs.

One can yet sense in reading the yellowed journals of Pleasant Hill the relief of the Shakers in the note, "Their hasty flight was hailed with joy by peaceable and non-resistant citizens, who had thus been rudely invaded, and frightened from their midnight repose; and grateful thanks were devoutly offered up for that Divine protection under whose hallowed influence no casualties had occurred. The balance of the night was spent in painful anxiety & dread, while the brethren patrolled the premises on guard. The ruffians robbed a near neighbor of about $300. No clue to the diabolical traitors."

The Civil War had an enormous impact on Pleasant Hill and its nonresistant Shakers. Like a cancerous disease it helped to start a slow deterioration in the Society. While it is true the total membership remained at a fairly steady count of approximately 320, there stirred in the community after 1865 a restlessness which the Order was never able to allay. Like their worldly Kentucky neighbors the Shakers had to go in search of new markets for their products. Their traditional southern customers were bankrupted by the war. Too, the machine age in post-war America gave the humble hand craftsmen and kitchen preservers serious competition. Shaker farming activities which had once been so efficient and progressive now lagged, and in time the Pleasant Hill Community did little more than sustain itself. No longer were the Shaker herds of cattle and sheep of prize winning quality, and Brother Rufus Bryant no longer appeared at the great livestock auctions. Perhaps the most serious blow of all was an ill-advised venture into debt which piled up ruinous obligations through the years.

In the more humane field the war was no respecter of religious and social ideals. Tragically the tranquility of the Pleasant Hill of Zion was ruthlessly destroyed. It was strategically located on the main passage where the two armies were to face each other in the struggle for the control of Kentucky. At a more elementary level the ragamuffin soldiers who swarmed about the kitchen doors of the village had no appreciation of the meaning of social or spiritual tranquility, or did they know of the dream that by the establishment of a pattern of social communion a tiny fragment of the American population could at least find a meaning of life which lay beyond the eternal surge toward progress.

The spacious cellars of the Family Houses stored large quantities of food but many times during the War were cleaned out feeding hungry soldiers.

Addendum

by

EARL D. WALLACE, *Chairman*

Board of Trustees of Shakertown at Pleasant Hill, Kentucky, Inc.

Readers of Dr. Clark's account of the highly emotional experiences of the Shakers during the Civil War period may be curious as to what has happened to the many sturdy and magnificent buildings which housed almost 500 members of the Shaker Society at the height of its prosperity prior to the Civil War. Others may wonder about when the Village was first established and why, and especially how long this celibate sect managed to survive.

The plan to restore this historic community and to acquire 2,200 acres of the original Shaker lands, including 4,000 feet of the Kentucky River Palisades, began in 1961 with the founding of SHAKERTOWN AT PLEASANT HILL, KENTUCKY, INC. as a nonprofit educational corporation.

Hundreds of contributions from individuals, foundations, and corporations in many States of the Nation together with a 40 year restoration construction loan by the Economic Development Administration of the U.S. Department of Commerce have enabled the corporation to bring Pleasant Hill back to a living and thriving community. Pleasant Hill not only attracts visitors from all States of the Nation, but adds a new dimension to the spirit of those who are active in the movement to preserve the dwindling remains of the Historic Heritage of our country.

In recognition of the authentic restoration of the Pleasant Hill community, the Honorable Rogers C. B. Morton, Secretary of the United States Department of the Interior has awarded to the Trustees of the nonprofit corporation the following Certificate

SHAKERTOWN AT PLEASANT HILL
has been designated a
NATIONAL HISTORIC LANDMARK
This site possesses national significance in commemorating the history of the United States of America.

Those who visit the Village will see Pleasant Hill restored to its appearance of pre-Civil War days. This includes a portion of 500 miles of the early stagecoach road which ran from Zanesville, Ohio, to connect with the Natchez Trace at Nashville. The restored half mile runs through the Village from the east end to the Shaker graveyard on the west.

Exhibits in the original buildings tell the story of the Life and Customs of the Shakers during the 105 year span of the Society.

The Trustees House provides distinctive Kentucky food including that from Shaker recipes taken from the original journals.

Overnight accommodations include more than 60 guest rooms in the original buildings, all air-conditioned and comfortably furnished in Shaker style with rockers, handwoven carpets and curtains, and AAA approved.

Covering the periods before and after that of Dr. Clark's "Pleasant Hill in the Civil War," a brief story of the Shakers at Pleasant Hill which was included in the tenth anniversary report to the "Friends of Shakertown" is repeated on the following pages.

THE SHAKERS AT PLEASANT HILL

Pleasant Hill was no ordinary Village for it was our heritage from a most unusual people, the Shaker Society at Pleasant Hill, a religious order of celibates who settled there in 1805. This was only 13 years after Kentucky became a state and 5 years before the Battle of Tippecanoe where many Kentuckians fought the Indians. Thomas Jefferson was President at the time.

It was 167 years ago when three Shaker missionaries settled on 107 acres on Shawnee Run, now Shaker Creek, seven miles from the fledging fort town of Harrodsburg, and a mile or so from the limestone Palisades of Kentucky River. They came from the mother colony of Shakers near Albany, New York, which had been established in 1774 by a religious order that had fled England to escape persecution for their unorthodox practice of worship. They believed that Christ had reappeared in the female person of their leader who was Mother Ann. Being confirmed celibates, they believed that sex was the source of all evil. They colonized orders in many rural areas in New England by receiving converts and adopting orphans.

At heart the Shakers were missionaries of their faith. In coming to Kentucky their timing was right for in the early 1800's the feeling across the country was that the moral fibre of the nation was falling apart amidst the rush West in the conquest for land, trade and fortune.

So it was when they first came to Kentucky in 1805 in the midst of the greatest upheaval of religious ferment the State has ever known. Days and days of revival meetings were common to many backwoods areas, the most famous of which was Cane Ridge in Bourbon County which the three missionaries visited on their first trip.

In the same year they settled on Shawnee Run and began to build at Pleasant Hill. Converts to their faith multiplied as did their land holdings. Within 30 years or so they had constructed some 20 or more major buildings and shops. Their land holdings exceeded 4,000 acres and almost 500 members were at work in the grain fields and orchards.

They built a sawmill powered by a waterfall, a grist mill, a linseed oil mill, a fulling mill for cloth, a broom factory and a print shop.

Then followed herb gardens so they could make their own medicines. The native mulberry trees led to a thriving silk production. Fruit preserves and jellies were produced in abundance and stored in the large cellars.

The Shakers at Pleasant Hill would have nothing but the finest of livestock and horses. Their breeding followed the best bloodlines. The common mule was rejected as being against the principle of natural procreation. They imported the Bakewell sheep from England. They attended livestock sales over the state and at times acted as judges at stock shows. In partnership with Henry Clay they owned "Orizimbo", one of the finest Durham bulls in Central Kentucky.

The Shakers were far in advance of their times in the skills and expertise of agriculture and livestock breeding and in the mechanical and architectural arts. Pleasant Hill was the early experiment station in Kentucky. In 1831, Robert Wickliffe, on the floor of the Kentucky Senate, made this recorded statement to his colleagues:

> Let a stranger visit your country, and inquire for your best specimens of agriculture, mechanics, and architecture, and sir, he is directed to visit the Society of Shakers at Pleasant Hill.

The Pleasant Hill Shakers were not only self-sufficient but developed down river trade all the way to New Orleans for their surpluses in farm produce, wool, silk, cloth, preserves, brooms and the finest of seeds. In fact their products were the hallmark of integrity in the marketplace.

As early as 1833 they put into operation the first town waterworks west of the Alleghenies and piped water to the kitchens and many of the stock barns. They made vegetable dyes for their wool and tanned leather for the cobbler who made shoes and boots for the members. They were imaginative and progressive in inventing labor-saving machinery on the farm and for the kitchens. While they led an austere life at work, they ate sumptuously at the table. In fact, so well that many hard scrabbling farmers around gave their land to the Society and moved to the security of the Village.

The Shakers were meticulous in recording the daily events at the Village and of their trading trips in Kentucky and in the south. The penmanship in their numerous journals looks like a steel engraving and their prose showed a fine command of language. They recorded an annual census of each family building, name and age. The large Center Family House at one time showed 92 people, male on one side of the house, and female on the other. An interesting journal entry was about one of their frequent trips to consult with Hector Hillenmeyer, an early horticulturist, near Lexington about fruit tree grafting. The architect builder at Pleasant Hill, Micajah Burnett, knew Rafinesque, the great Turkish-born naturalist at Transylvania College. In fact, Rafinesque left a pencil drawing of his friend's profile which has been published a time or two.

The Pleasant Hill Shakers were avid readers of farm journals and newspapers and had widespread contacts in the south through their customers along the Mississippi. In the 1850's the Shakers began to record in ominous tones the rumblings of secession and war. While they were pacifists and neutral in political questions, they sensed the consequences of a war in Kentucky. Their bins were full of grain, cellars stored with food, and their fine herds of cattle and horses grazed about.

Then came the Civil War in Kentucky with father against son, and brother against brother as editorialized in the Kentucky papers. Distress and concern possessed this quiet and peaceful Village of religious people.

Fighting for control of Central Kentucky, both armies passed back and forth on the main stagecoach road through Pleasant Hill demanding to be fed and to be supplied with wagons, horses, and beef cattle. The ravages of 4 years of war took its toll and the society began a 40 year decline. In 1910 only a dozen elderly sisters survived to deed the property to a friend to care for them; the last one died in 1923.

April, 1863.

19 The scarlet fever still prevails at the Center Family. Joanne (Jane) Balbance deceased there this morning, in her 87th year since the 6th ult. She had been unusually hale & sprightly for one of her age. She was among the first of them who embraced the truth in this western country, and has been an industrious, faithful soul in support of the cause ever since, & now goes to enjoy the happy fruits of her long & well spent life. Her funeral took place at half past five this evening at the Center Family, the other Families not attending, lest the disease might spread among them.

22 We had about an inch rain last night, just in time for vegetation though early fruit is in bloom, but if the rain now ceases it is not probable they will be much damaged.

23 A light shower last night, but clear & warm today.

26 The orchards and shrubberies are now a perfect garland of flowers & fine growing weather, though the nights are some cool yet no frost. A splendid prospect for fruit if old Boreas will not be too greedy.

27 Sally Hooser deceased at the East Family after several years of confinement under affliction, and would have been ninety years of age on this day (Monday) next week. She was one of those pioneers that early embraced the faith, having believed Oct 1809, and been a faithful & devoted servant in the cause ever since. J. R. Bryant went to Louisville & E. W. Scott to Lebanon, trading. Adelaide Anderson was taken from the W. F. to the world by her mother.

29 E. W. Scott returned from Lebanon. See the 27th inst

30 Thursday   **Prayer Day.**

This day was appointed by Abraham Lincoln, President of the United States, to be observed by the nation as a day of fasting, prayer & humiliation, on account of the relentless & cruel war that is now raging & filling the land with ruin & desolation. We, in this Society, k the day according to our usual custom. We occupied the morning to 9½ o'clock cleaning & righting up the premises &c. And then gathered